FESTIVALS! USA

Mardi Gras
A City's Masked Parade

Lisa Gabbert

The Rosen Publishing Group's
PowerKids Press™
New York

To Bill, my Rex.

Published in 1999 by The Rosen Publishing Group, Inc.
29 East 21st Street, New York, NY 10010

First Edition

Book Design: Michael de Guzman

Photo Credits: pp. 4, 16 © Frank Gordon/FPG International; p. 7 © Farrell Grehan/FPG International; p. 8 © Corbis-Bettmann; pp. 11, 15, 20 © Suzanne A. Vlamis/International Stock; p. 12 © George Ancona/ International Stock; p. 19 © J. Pickerell/FPG International.

Gabbert, Lisa.
    Mardi Gras: a city's masked parade / Lisa Gabbert.
        p.   cm. — (Festivals! USA)
    Includes index.
    Summary: Describes the origins, symbols, and celebration of the pre-Lenten festivities held each year in New Orleans, Louisiana, and popularly known as Mardi Gras.
    ISBN 0-8239-5337-8
    1. Carnival—Juvenile literature. 2. Carnival—Louisiana—Juvenile literature. 3. New Orleans (La.)—Social life and customs—Juvenile literature. [1. Mardi Gras.] I. Title. II. Series.
GT4180.G32   1998
394.25—dc21   98-3526
                                                       CIP
                                                       AC

Manufactured in the United States of America

Contents

Mardi Gras and Lent

Mardi Gras is a holiday that doesn't always happen on the same date each year. Its date depends on the Christian holiday of Easter. The 40 days before Easter are called Lent. For many Catholic people, Lent is a serious, special time when they prepare for Easter. Many years ago, people wanted to have fun before Lent began, so the six weeks before Lent are a time of **celebration** (sel-uh-BRAY-shun) called **carnival** (KAR-nih-vul). During carnival, people celebrate with parades, parties, feasts, and costumed dances. Mardi Gras is the last day of carnival.

◀ *Mardi Gras is celebrated at the end of carnival, with parades and parties.*

Fat Tuesday

Mardi Gras is French for "fat Tuesday." Sometimes it is called Shrove Tuesday or Pancake Tuesday. Fat Tuesday is the day before Ash Wednesday, which is the first day of Lent. One story says that the day is called fat Tuesday because Catholics had to use up their butter and other fatty foods by this day. Catholics of the past were not allowed to eat butter, fat, or meat during Lent. Today, Mardi Gras also means carnival and refers to the celebrations that are held during this time.

One of the biggest Mardi Gras celebrations ▶
happens in New Orleans, Louisiana.

Mardi Gras in New Orleans

The state of Louisiana was once a French and Spanish **colony** (KOL-uh-nee). Carnival was very popular in France and Spain. The **descendants** (dee-SEN-dents) of French and Spanish settlers were called **Creoles** (KREE-ohlz). Many Creoles enjoyed having costumed dances and parades on carnival, just like those in France and Spain. The modern Mardi Gras began in New Orleans in 1827. That year, on fat Tuesday, young men wearing bright costumes marched through the streets. A **tradition** (truh-DIH-shun) was born.

◀ *Mardi Gras has been celebrated in the United States for more than 100 years.*

Costumes and Dancing

Dancing and costumes have always been important in New Orleans, and balls were often held in the colony of New Orleans. Mardi Gras begins with the Twelfth Night Reveler's Ball. This is the twelfth day after Christmas. More than 60 formal dances are held during the carnival season. Some dances have **themes** (THEEMZ), and people wear masks and costumes. People dress as fairies, animals, and characters from **myths** (MITHS) and religions.

Many different costumes can be seen during ▸
Mardi Gras, such as these medieval outfits.

Mardi Gras Krewes

A **krewe** (KROO) is a carnival club. There are many krewes in New Orleans. Krewes plan different parts of Mardi Gras, such as parades and host dances. Some krewes, like the Krewe of Comus, are over 140 years old. The oldest krewes are very powerful and plan Mardi Gras. The Captain of one krewe is the head of all of the clubs. He rides in a place of **honor** (ON-er) in the krewe's parade.

◀ *Some krewes like to dress in matching costumes during Mardi Gras.*

Mardi Gras Kings and Queens

Each krewe elects a king and queen. For example, King Comus never takes off his mask. Nobody knows who he is. The head king is called Rex, which means "king" in Latin. Rex first appeared in Mardi Gras celebrations in 1872. Rex and his queen still rule the Mardi Gras festival today. They have a special flag that is purple, green, and gold. Sometimes Rex arrives at Mardi Gras by boat and is saluted by cannons.

The arrival of a krewe's king and queen ▶ is a big part of the parade.

The Mardi Gras Parades

The parades are an important part of Mardi Gras, and there are between 60 and 70 of them each year. In the past, there was a **masquerade** (mas-kuh-RAYD) in the streets and people decorated their carriages. Today, most krewes host parades with a special theme. People ride parade floats and wear costumes that are part of the theme. There can be more than 30 floats. Themes come from history, mythology, **legends** (LEH-jendz), and **literature** (LIT-er-uh-chur). The parades last for twelve days.

The detail and attention in the making of Mardi Gras floats can be seen as they roll through the parade.

Throw Me Something, Mister!

Each year during Mardi Gras, the streets of New Orleans fill with thousands of people. They shout "Throw me something, mister!" to the costumed people who ride the floats or march in the parades. The people in the parades toss "throws." Throws are colored plastic beads, cups decorated with krewe **emblems** (EM-blemz), coins called **doubloons** (duh-BLOONZ), and other small things. Throws aren't worth a lot of money, but people still like to collect them.

Each year, people come from all over the world to New Orleans's Mardi Gras. ▶

All in Good Fun

Part of Mardi Gras is making fun of other people. This is done by dressing up like these people and imitating them, which is called **parody** (PAYR-uh-dee). In 1909, some African Americans crowned their own king of Mardi Gras, who they called the King of the Zulus. This king made fun of Rex by wearing a can for a crown and by carrying a banana stalk. The King of the Zulus became a very big Mardi Gras figure. In 1949, the famous jazz musician Louis Armstrong was the Zulu King.

The parodies that take place during Mardi Gras, such as this one of the King of the Zulus, are always just for fun.

A Worldwide Festival

Mardi Gras has become a very popular celebration for people all over the world. Cities such as Cologne and Nice in France and Rio de Janeiro in Brazil all celebrate this colorful festival. People spend all year making their costumes. Some costumes have ostrich feathers, rhinestones, **sequins** (SEE-kwinz), **papier-mâché** (PAY-per muh-SHAY), or beads. Some headdresses are over four feet high! Mardi Gras is a time for people to have fun and think about the time ahead of them.

Glossary

carnival (KAR-nih-vul) A time of celebration and fun before Lent.

celebration (sel-uh-BRAY-shun) A special time held in honor of something.

colony (KOL-uh-nee) An area in a new country where a large group of people move, but who remain under the rule of their own country.

Creole (KREE-ohl) A distant relative of French and Spanish settlers.

descendant (dee-SEN-dent) A person born of a certain family or group.

doubloon (duh-BLOON) A fake coin that is thrown during Mardi Gras parades.

emblem (EM-blem) A symbol or other figure used as an identifying mark.

honor (ON-er) Respect and admiration from others.

krewe (KROO) A carnival club that is in charge of a certain part of Mardi Gras.

legend (LEH-jend) A story that comes from the past and is still told today.

literature (LIT-er-uh-chur) The writings of a certain country or period of time.

masquerade (mas-kuh-RAYD) A party or dance at which costumes and masks are worn.

myth (MITH) A story that explains something in nature.

papier-mâché (PAY-per muh-SHAY) Paper mixed with water to make a paste that can be molded when wet. When it dries, it becomes hard and strong.

parody (PAYR-uh-dee) To make fun of someone by imitating him or her.

sequins (SEE-kwinz) Very small metal or plastic discs used to decorate clothing.

theme (THEEM) A subject or topic.

tradition (truh-DIH-shun) A way of doing something that is passed down through a family.

Index